Your Life in Christ

NAVPRESS⬤.

NavPress is the publishing ministry of The Navigators, an international Christian organization and leader in personal spiritual development. NavPress is committed to helping people grow spiritually and enjoy lives of meaning and hope through personal and group resources that are biblically rooted, culturally relevant, and highly practical.

For a free catalog go to www.NavPress.com
or call 1.800.366.7788 in the United States or 1.800.839.4769 in Canada.

ISBN 978-1-60006-004-5

Cover design by Arvid Wallen
Cover illustration by Michael Halbert
Interior design by The DesignWorks Group
Creative Team: Dan Rich, Arvid Wallen, Darla Hightower, Pamela Poll, Pat Reinheimer, Kathy Guist

Original DFD Author: Chuck Broughton
Revision Team: Dennis Stokes, Judy Gomoll, Christine Weddle, Ralph Ennis

Printed in the United States of America

6 7 8 9 10 11 / 13 12 11 10 09

DFD1 | CONTENTS

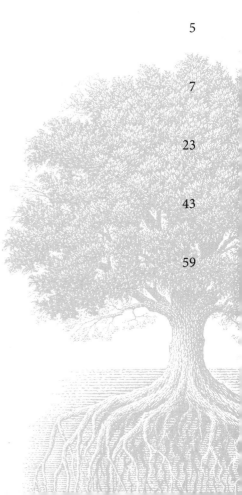

NOT BY BREAD ALONE

Billions of the world's people go through life spiritually undernourished. The words Jesus spoke centuries ago are still true — "Man does not live on bread alone, but on every word that comes from the mouth of God" (Matthew 4:4).

Because they recognize this need in their lives that only God can satisfy, many people are turning to serious study of the Bible. Everyone needs to study the Bible — both those new to faith in Jesus and those who have known Christ for many years.

The *Design for Discipleship* studies have been carefully planned to help you:

- *Establish a program of personal study of the Scriptures.*
- *Examine the great truths of the Bible and your response to these.*
- *Learn and practice the essentials of discipleship.*

To get the full benefit of the course, it is important to work consecutively from Book One through Book Seven.

All you need to begin is a Bible. Each question will direct you to a passage of Scripture. After thinking about the passage, write the answer in your own words.

Scripture references will give the book, chapter, and verse. For example, Revelation 3:20 refers to the book of Revelation, chapter 3, verse 20.

Be sure to pray before you begin each chapter. Ask the Lord for understanding as you study these topics:

- *God Cares for You*
- *The Person of Jesus Christ*
- *The Work of Christ*
- *The Spirit Within You*

At the end of each chapter you will also have an opportunity to process your ideas and feelings. Feel free to use it for:

- **questions** *you still have*
- **responses** *that were significant to you*
- **creative expressions** *(poetry, drawing)*
- **journaling**
- **going deeper** *into the topic*
- **summary** *of thoughts and feelings*

You are in for an adventure as you deepen in your life with Christ.

1

God Cares for You

You are a special person. You are special because God says you are valuable to Him. He genuinely cares about you and what happens to you.

In this chapter you will investigate four statements of God's concern for you:

- *God created you.*
- *God is present and knows you.*
- *God loves you.*
- *God adopted you into His family.*

GOD CREATED YOU

BEGINNINGS. The most amazing ones flow from God's cosmic plan and design. God Himself is infinite and amazing. Power. Knowledge. Creativity.

1. The first chapter of the Bible tells us that God created the universe out of nothingness. Read Genesis 1:1-5 and list at least three things you notice concerning the Creation.

2. Through what forces did God create the world? (Hebrews 11:3)

3. Out of God's infinite wisdom and capacity, He designed and created you. Why? (Isaiah 43:7)

4. The dignity God gave human beings is shown by a person's uniqueness, authority, and purpose. List some ideas from Genesis 1:26-28 that indicate:

a. The uniqueness of humankind

b. The position or authority of humankind

c. God's purpose for humankind

5. Do you like being part of God's humankind? Why or why not?

6. How do you respond to God as your Creator?
   (Revelation 4:11)

GOD IS PRESENT AND KNOWS YOU

7. In Psalm 139:1-8, David mentions several areas of his personal
   life that God has "searched and known." List at least four of them.
   Then place a check mark by the areas you think God knows about
   your life.

> Grace means there is nothing I can do to make God love me more, and nothing I can do to make God love me less. It means that I, even I who deserve the opposite, am invited to take my place at the table in God's family.

> —Philip Yancey,
> *What's So Amazing About Grace?*

8. How did David respond as he realized that God knew him completely and that God is present everywhere? (Psalm 139:23-24)

9. How do you feel about God's detailed interest in you as revealed by Jesus? (Matthew 10:29-31)

10. What was God's greatest demonstration of His love?
    (1 John 4:9-10)

GOD SO LOVED THE WORLD...

WHOEVER BELIEVES IN HIM

shall not perish

but have
everlasting life

DEATH ──────→ LIFE

HE GAVE HIS ONLY SON JESUS

11. Study John 3:16 in relationship to the previous illustration.

a. What motivated God to sacrifice His Son for us?

b. How can a person respond to God's offer of eternal life?

> Jesus offers himself as God's doorway into the life
> that is truly life. Confidence in him leads us today, as
> in other times, to become his apprentices in eternal
> living. "Those who come through me will be safe,"
> he said. "They will go in and out and find all they
> need. I have come into their world that they may
> have life, and life to the limit."
>
> —Dallas Willard,
> *The Divine Conspiracy*

12. In John 10:9-16, Jesus uses metaphorical language by comparing His love and concern to the love and concern of a shepherd. According to this passage, what are some of the ways Jesus cares for us?

13. Do you feel worthy to receive God's love? Is receiving love easy for you? Why or why not?

14. Do you think God requires you to be worthy of love or feel worthy of love before He loves you? Explain.

Thank God for all the things you listed in question 12. Praise Him that these things are given to you because of Jesus and that you do not earn them by your actions.

15. How do you feel about addressing God as Jesus described in Matthew 6:9?

16. Is it true that God is everyone's Father? Why or why not? (John 8:42-44)

17. How is one born into God's family? (John 1:12-13)

Consider writing a brief letter or prayer to God expressing your feelings to Him as your Father.

> **"** The importance of the assurance of faith lies in the fact that, childlike, I cannot possibly love or serve God if I do not know whether he loves and acknowledges me as his child.
>
> —Andrew Murray, *The New Life*

18. From Romans 8:15-17 what are some blessings of being adopted as a true child of God? From these blessings circle the one that touches your heart most.

Finish this comparison:
Being born into God's family is like . . .

19. Describe briefly where you
    are in the journey of knowing
    God as your Father (*Abba* is a
    personal name for father).

It is important for you as a follower of Jesus to be assured that God is your Father and that you have eternal life. Although emotions are important in any relationship, they can change for many reasons. So our assurance of being in God's family must ultimately depend on the word of God, who is trustworthy and keeps His promises. "I write these things to you who believe . . . that you may know that you have eternal life" (1 John 5:13).

The following verses have helped many gain this assurance. Consider memorizing one of them to strengthen your assurance.

"I tell you the truth, whoever hears my word and believes him who sent me has eternal life and will not be condemned; he has crossed over from death to life." (John 5:24)

And this is the testimony: God has given us eternal life, and this life is in his Son. He who has the Son has life; he who does not have the Son of God does not have life. (1 John 5:11-12)

"Here I am! I stand at the door and knock. If anyone hears my voice and opens the door, I will come in and eat with him, and he with me." (Revelation 3:20)

Remember, this is an opportunity to process and creatively express your ideas and feelings. Feel free to use it for: **questions** you still have, **responses** that were significant to you, a **summary** of your thoughts and feelings, or a **creative expression.**

► God created you for His own purpose and His glory. He gave you dignity by shaping you after His own likeness.

► God considers you to be of great value. Our ever-present Father takes personal interest in knowing you completely.

► He loves you so intensely that He sent His Son to die for you on the cross. This demonstration of His love shows He wants to give you an eternal and abundant life.

► When God gave you this life in Jesus Christ, you were spiritually born into God's family. He is your Father. You are His child. He cares for you!

> God notices you. The fact is he can't take his eyes off of you. However badly you think of yourself, God is in love with you. Some of us even fear that someday we'll do something so bad that he won't notice us anymore. Well, let me tell you. God loves you completely. . . and in the love of God there are no degrees, there is only love.
>
> —Rich Mullins

What is your earthly father like? Do you like him? Explain.

What is our perfect heavenly Father like? How much do you like Him?

How do you think your feelings about your earthly father have affected how you feel about your heavenly Father? Explain.

The Person of Jesus Christ

Man just isn't capable of fully understanding God. God is perfect and holy, while man is morally flawed and sinful. To bridge the gap and to connect God and man, God took the form of a man in Jesus Christ.

Jesus Christ is "the image of the invisible God. . . . For God was pleased to have all his fullness dwell in him" (Colossians 1:15,19). That's what *deity* means — that Jesus Christ was God Himself.

To be the complete expression of God, Christ had to be God. To be seen and understood by man, He had to be human. Jesus Christ has a dual nature — He is the God-man.

In order to begin understanding Jesus Christ, it is necessary to explore His deity and His humanity.

THE DEITY OF
JESUS CHRIST

Was Jesus Christ just a great man? To some He was the founder of a new religion. Others consider Him a prophet. But Jesus Himself claimed that He was God.

He also authenticated that He was God. If this claim were not true, He could not be called even a good man, but would be an imposter and a liar.

1. The writer of Hebrews describes Christ's deity in chapter 1. Read Hebrews 1 before answering questions 1-4. Jesus' superiority to the angels is shown by:

Verses 4-5

Verse 6

Verses 13-14

2. Look again at Hebrews 1:8-12. In the blank next to each statement below, write the number of the verse that brings out the truth stated.

Jesus is the Creator _____

Jesus is unchangeable _____

Jesus is eternal _____

Jesus is righteous _____

3. In Hebrews 1:3 what encourages you about Jesus' ability to reveal God?

4. How does God view Jesus in Hebrews 1:8 and 1:10?

5. From John 10:27-30, what does Jesus promise to those who follow Him? How does that make you feel?

6. While on earth, Jesus performed many miracles that clearly demonstrated His divine power. From the following verses in Matthew 8, list the ways Jesus showed supernatural power.

Verse 3

Verses 6,13

Verses 16-17

Verses 23-27

7. Imagine that you were there to see
Jesus performing these miracles. How
would you describe to a friend what
happened?

8. Read John 11:38-44. How do you think this unique unleashing of Jesus' power affected those who were there?

9. After observing Jesus' life, power, and preaching, what did Peter conclude about Him? (Matthew 16:13-16)

And later in Acts 4:12?

10. Jesus was born, lived, died, rose from the dead, and ascended back into heaven. But what is He doing today and into the future? Consider the passages below as you reflect on Jesus today.

Romans 8:34

Philippians 2:9-11

Revelation 5:11-12

11. Review questions 1-10. Give three reasons why you believe Jesus
    Christ is God.

12. How is Jesus' humanity seen in the following situations?

John 4:6

John 4:7

John 11:35

13. The chart on pages 32-33 illustrates how Jesus fulfilled prophecy. How do the verses in this chart influence your concept of who Jesus is?

14. Matthew 4:1-11 is the account of a series of temptations Jesus faced.

    a. In each of His three answers to Satan, Jesus used the same phrase.

       What is it?

       What does it mean?

Prophecies About Jesus Christ

Fulfilled prophecy helps verify the truth that Jesus is the Christ, the Son of God. Even though these prophecies preceded Jesus by hundreds of years, Jesus fulfilled them in every detail — proving that His claims were authentic. The following chart is a brief list of some of the prophecies made concerning the Christ and how Jesus fulfilled them.

Topic	Prophecy	Fulfillment
Place of birth	"But you, Bethlehem Ephrathah, though you are small among the clans of Judah, out of you will come for me one who will be ruler over Israel, whose origins are from of old, from ancient times" (Micah 5:2), 700 BC.	"Jesus was born in Bethlehem in Judea" (Matthew 2:1).
Born of a virgin	"The virgin will be with child and will give birth to a son, and will call him Immanuel" (Isaiah 7:14), 700 BC.	"His mother Mary was pledged to be married to Joseph, but before they came together, she was found to be with child through the Holy Spirit" (Matthew 1:18).
His triumphal entry	"Rejoice greatly, O Daughter of Zion! Shout, Daughter of Jerusalem! See, your king comes to you, righteous and having salvation, gentle and riding on a donkey, on a colt, the foal of a donkey" (Zechariah 9:9), 500 BC.	"They took palm branches and went out to meet him, shouting, 'Hosanna! Blessed is he who comes in the name of the Lord! Blessed is the King of Israel!' Jesus found a young donkey and sat upon it" (John 12:13-14).

Betrayed by a friend	"Even my close friend, whom I trusted, he who shared my bread, has lifted up his heel against me" (Psalm 41:9), 1000 BC.	"Then Judas Iscariot, one of the Twelve, went to the chief priests to betray Jesus to them" (Mark 14:10).
His rejection	"He was despised and rejected by men … Like one from whom men hide their faces he was despised, and we esteemed him not" (Isaiah 53:3), 700 BC.	"He came to that which was his own, but his own did not receive him" (John 1:11).
Crucified with sinners	"He … was numbered with the transgressors" (Isaiah 53:12), 700 BC.	"Two robbers were crucified with him, one on his right and one on his left" (Matthew 27:38).
Hands and feet pierced	"They have pierced my hands and my feet" (Psalm 22:16), 1000 BC.	"Put your finger here; see my hands. Reach out your hand and put it into my side" (John 20:27).
His resurrection	"You will not abandon me to the grave, nor will you let your Holy One see decay" (Psalm 16:10), 1000 BC.	"You killed the author of life, but God raised him from the dead" (Acts 3:15).
His ascension	"You ascended on high" (Psalm 68:18), 1000 BC.	"He was taken up before their very eyes, and a cloud hid him from their sight" (Acts 1:9).

b. Draw lines to connect the verses in Matthew 4 with the corresponding verses in Deuteronomy.

Matthew 4:4   Deuteronomy 6:13

Matthew 4:7   Deuteronomy 6:16

Matthew 4:10   Deuteronomy 8:3

c. What is one temptation you often face?

d. How can you follow Jesus' example and arm yourself against this temptation?

- Thank God that He understands what it is to be tempted.
- Ask Him to help you overcome this temptation.
- When you fail, be sure to claim His promise:
  "If we confess our sins, he is faithful and just
  and will forgive us our sins and purify us from
  all unrighteousness" (1 John 1:9).
- Thank Him for His mercy.

15. Read Hebrews 4:15-16.

   a. What did Jesus experience that is common to man?
      (verse 15)

   b. How do you feel about Jesus being able to relate to your pain,
      temptations, and sufferings? (verse 16)

c. What are the benefits of Jesus sharing the human experience with us? (verse 16)

> Either this man was, and is, the Son of God: or else a madman or something worse. But don't let us come with any patronizing nonsense about his being a great human teacher. He hasn't left that open to us. He didn't intend to.
>
> —C. S. Lewis

16. Who do you think Jesus is? (Check all that apply.)

_____ a good man

_____ a good but dead man

_____ a prophet and teacher

_____ a man raised from the dead

_____ a god-like man

_____ the Son of God

_____ the Savior of humankind

_____ the Author and Finisher of our faith

_____ our brother

_____ (other) _____

17. Jesus claimed to be equal with God in what ways?

John 5:19,20   Equal in working

John 5:21,28-29   Equal in resurrecting power

John 5:22,27

John 5:23

John 5:24-25

John 5:26   Equal in self-existence

> Jesus Christ became incarnate for one purpose, to
> make a way back to God that man might stand
> before him as he was created to do, the friend and
> lover of God himself.
>
> —Oswald Chambers

18. What questions, doubts, or issues with Jesus do you have that you would still like to resolve?

19. Read John 20:24-29. What happened to Thomas (sometimes called the doubter) when he saw Jesus after He had risen from the dead?

> ❝ Wandering in a sea of relativism, we find there *is* truth, and the truth is Jesus. Jesus not only *preached* the good news; he *is* the good news. This truth is not religious dogma, an institution, or even religion. Truth is a person. We gain hold of what is true through grabbing hold of Jesus, the author of truth.
>
> —Jonathan S. Campbell with Jennifer Campbell,
> *The Way of Jesus: A Journey of Freedom*
> *for Pilgrims and Wanderers*

Where are you now in your discovery journey regarding Jesus?

▶ Jesus Christ is the perfect image of God. As God, He has authority over the earth and angels.

▶ Jesus was human, too. Many of His experiences were similar to those you have today. He suffered and was tempted. Though He never yielded, this allows Him to understand and be merciful when you are tempted. When you fail, He forgives as you confess your sins to Him (1 John 1:9).

Meditate on Hebrews 2:11. Why do you think Jesus is not ashamed to be of the same family with us? Have you ever felt ashamed of being a follower of Jesus? Explain.

Jesus described Himself as one who would meet a wide variety of needs. Think about the passages below and then respond to what these aspects of Jesus can mean to you.

Reference	How Jesus Refers to Himself	Meaning to Your Life
John 4:10-14	The living water	
John 6:32-35	The bread of life	
John 8:12	The light of the world	
John 10:7-10	The door	
John 10:11-18	The good shepherd	
John 11:17-27, 32-44	The resurrection and the life	
John 14:1-7	The way, the truth, and the life	
John 15:1-17	The true vine	

3

The Work of Christ

Many have heard about the last events of Jesus' life on earth—sometimes called the Passion of the Christ. He was falsely accused, tried, and condemned. Then He suffered as a common criminal, hung from a cross until dead, and three days later rose from the dead. But few people understand the meaning of these events. In this chapter, you will explore Jesus' life, His death, and His resurrection—and what it all means.

THE LIFE OF JESUS CHRIST

About 2,000 years ago, Jesus was born in the obscure town of Bethlehem. While Jesus was an infant, Joseph and Mary took Him into Egypt to escape the wrath of King Herod the Great. Then, while He was still a young child, they moved to a small town called Nazareth in the region of Galilee, in the land now called Israel.

1. When the angel announced His birth, what purpose did he give for Jesus coming into the world? (Matthew 1:21; Luke 1:31-33)

2. At the age of thirty, after working with His father Joseph as a carpenter, Jesus began His public ministry. What are some activities of Jesus' public ministry? (Matthew 4:23)

3. Jesus did not fulfill His ministry alone. According to Mark 3:14, what was His purpose in selecting twelve men to live and minister with Him? What criteria do you think Jesus may have used for selecting these twelve?

4. Read Luke 22:25-27. How did Jesus expect His disciples to live?

What would it look like for you to live the same way today?

5. Just before Jesus was crucified, He reframed His relationship with the disciples. He called them friends (see John 15:15). As you reflect on Jesus' life, is He someone you would have gravitated to as a friend? Do you wish to be His friend today? Explain.

This study merely touches on some of the recorded events of Jesus' life. At the end of the Gospel of John we read, "Jesus did many other things as well. If every one of them were written down, I suppose that even the whole world would not have room for the books that would be written" (John 21:25). Some of the more familiar events of Jesus' life are presented in the illustration on page 47.

THE DEATH OF JESUS CHRIST

6. Both the Old Testament prophecies and Jesus Himself predicted His death (see Luke 18:31-33). Read Matthew 27:34-44. Briefly describe His death, including what was happening around Jesus then and how you think He suffered.

AN OVERVIEW OF THE LIFE OF CHRIST

Birth	DEVELOPING YEARS		CARPENTER	PUBLIC MINISTRY
2		12		30	33

Birth
- Birth in Bethlehem
- Flight to Egypt
- Move to Galilee

- Visit to the Temple
- Discussion with Rabbis

THREE YEARS OF PUBLIC MINISTRY

30	31	32	33 LAST WEEK

- Baptized by John
- Tempted in the Wilderness
- First Miracle: Water to Wine
- First Passover: Cast Out the Moneychangers
- Woman at the Well

- Second Passover
- Calling of the 12
- Sermon on the Mount
- Parable of the Sower
- Gadarene Demoniac Healed

- 12 Apostles Commissioned
- Feeding the 5000
- Jesus Walks on Water
- Transfiguration
- 70 Sent Out on Evangelism
- Raising Lazarus from the Dead

THE LAST WEEK

Arrival at Jerusalem	Final Days of Ministry	Crucified	Risen
• Triumphal Entry into Jerusalem • Casting Moneychangers out of the Temple	• Great Commandment: Love • Signs of Coming Events • Plot of Jews and Judas • Passover Meal, Wash Disciples' Feet • Lord's Supper • True Vine • Intercessory Prayer • Betrayal	• Trials before High Priest, Council, Pilate and Herod • Death: Crucifixion, Burial	• Resurrection • Appear to Disciples • Appear to 500 • Ascension

7. According to John 10:17-18, did Jesus go to the cross voluntarily? Explain your answer.

8. Read 1 Peter 3:18 and John 3:18-19. Why do you think Jesus had to come and die?

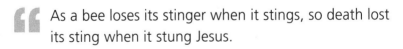 As a bee loses its stinger when it stings, so death lost its sting when it stung Jesus.

—Dennis Stokes

9. Read 1 Corinthians 15:55-57. What happened to the power of death because of Jesus?

10. Does the death of Jesus seem necessary and/or fair to you? How does your answer affect the way you approach your relationship with God?

THE RESURRECTION OF JESUS CHRIST

11. After Jesus died and was buried, what was done to secure His tomb? (Matthew 27:62-66)

12. Read Matthew 28:1-7. What was discovered at the tomb on the first day of the week? What did the angel say about Jesus?

13. What were the soldiers bribed to say? (Matthew 28:11-15)

> As a lawyer I have made a prolonged study of the evidences for the events of the first Easter Day. To me the evidence is conclusive, and over and over again in the High Court I have secured the verdict on evidence not nearly so compelling. . . . I accept [the Gospel evidence for the resurrection] unreservedly as the testimony of truthful men to facts they were able to substantiate.
>
> —Edward Clarke, quoted in *Basic Christianity*

14. After His resurrection, Christ appeared to His disciples.

   a. What was their first impression? (Luke 24:36-37)

   b. What things did He do to show them He had a body?
      (Luke 24:39-43)

15. Throughout the centuries, many people have tried to deny and disprove the resurrection of Jesus, while Christians believe that it is at the very center of their faith.

   a. Read 1 Corinthians 15:14-19. If Christ was not raised from the dead, then what? What are some implications?

b. Now read 1 Corinthians 15:20-26. If Christ was truly raised from the dead, then what? What are some implications?

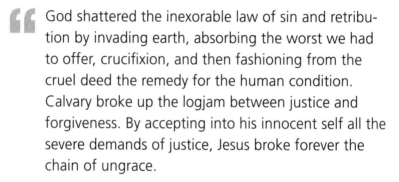

God shattered the inexorable law of sin and retribution by invading earth, absorbing the worst we had to offer, crucifixion, and then fashioning from the cruel deed the remedy for the human condition. Calvary broke up the logjam between justice and forgiveness. By accepting into his innocent self all the severe demands of justice, Jesus broke forever the chain of ungrace.

—Philip Yancey, *What's So Amazing About Grace?*

16. Hebrews 12:1-3. What do you think motivated Jesus to endure the agony of betrayal and shame and death? What does this mean to you?

17. What does it mean to you to know
    that Jesus was raised from death and is
    alive today?

18. What is the essence of the gospel message and the hope it gives
    you? (1 Corinthians 15:1-5)

Over this past week, how has the reality of Jesus influenced your life? Explain.

► Jesus Christ was born in Bethlehem, raised in Galilee, and became a carpenter. He spent three years ministering to thousands and proving that He was the Christ.

► Then He was condemned to die on a cross to bear the penalty for our sin.

► After three days, Jesus rose bodily from the dead. His resurrection is a historical reality.

The Bible describes Jesus' resurrection as a historical fact that happened in real time. From these passages, notice who saw Jesus after God raised Him from death.

WITNESS to the RESURRECTED JESUS

Reference	Place	Witnesses Who Saw Jesus After His Death
John 21:14-17	Tomb	Mary of Magdala
Matthew 28:8-9	Leaving tomb	Women
Luke:24:36-43	Jerusalem	Eleven disciples
John 20:24-31	A house	Thomas
Matthew 28:16-17	Galilee (mountain)	Eleven disciples
Luke 24:13-35	Road to Emmaus	Cleopas and friend
John 21:13-35	Sea of Tiberias	Disciples
1 Corinthians 15:5	(around Jerusalem?)	Peter
1 Corinthians 15:6	(around Jerusalem?)	500 brethren
1 Corinthians 15:7	(around Jerusalem?)	James
1 Corinthians 15:8	On the road to Damascus	Saul (renamed Paul)

How does this help deepen your confidence in a living Jesus?

The Spirit Within You

Jesus rose from the dead — and now He lives! When He ascended into heaven, the angels predicted that He would come back again some day (Acts 1:9-11). But in the meantime, He did not leave His followers alone. He sent them the Holy Spirit — another person within the Triune God — so that all followers of Christ might enjoy His presence 24/7 and live under His transformative influence and control.

THE COMING OF
THE HOLY SPIRIT

1. As Jesus tried to prepare His disciples for His death, how were they feeling about their future? (John 14:1,18)

2. What did Jesus ask His Father to do to comfort the disciples? (John 14:16,26)

3. Jesus' work and influence on earth did not end at His death and ascension — it was just getting started! What were some things Jesus promised He would keep on doing for His followers after He returned to heaven?

   John 14: 1-2

John 14:3-4

John 14:13-14

John 14:19

John 14:23

John 14:27

John 14:29

Why did Jesus promise them all these things?

JESUS' WORK TODAY

4. Read Ephesians 1:20-23. Where is Jesus today, and what is He doing?

What does this mean to you personally?

To *intercede* means "to plead on behalf of another."

5. What else is Christ doing for us now? (Romans 8:34)

6. In Jesus' great prayer recorded in John 17, what were some of the things He asked for His followers?

Verse 13

Verse 15

Verse 17

Verse 21

Verse 24

7. Do you think Jesus is praying the same things for you today? Read Hebrews 7:24-25. Explain your answer.

> Jesus is alive today! He reigns in heaven. He is active. He prays for us and perfects our faith. He is not an "un-dead."
>
> —Dennis Stokes

8. What else is Jesus doing today? Read Ephesians 5:25-27. How have you experienced Jesus making you holy and blameless?

The Persons of the Godhead never work separately.
Every act of God is done by all three Persons.

—A. W. Tozer

THE INDWELLING OF
THE HOLY SPIRIT

9. What is true of every believer?

Romans 8:9

1 Corinthians 2:12

1 Corinthians 3:16

Titus 3:5-6

How do you respond in your heart to this?

10. Why does God send His Spirit to indwell the believer? Circle the
    letter of the correct answer. (Galatians 4:6)

    a. Because the believer has been baptized.

    b. Because the believer is His child.

    c. Because the believer has dedicated his life to Him.

    d. Because the believer has had a special experience.

11. What are some results of the Holy Spirit's presence in the life of the believer? (2 Timothy 1:7)

THE LEADING OF THE HOLY SPIRIT

12. Galatians 5:16-17 describes the conflict in our lives

between _____ and

_____.

Who should control your life?

Here is one illustration of the power which results from the union of the Holy Spirit with the believer:

> I have in my hand a piece of lead. I hold it over a pool of water, and relax my grip. The lead is drawn irresistibly earthwards and sinks to the bottom of the pool. It has been mastered by the law of gravitation. I take the same piece of lead, attach it to a piece of wood, and drop it into the pool. Now it floats. No change has taken place in the nature or tendency of the lead, nor has the law of gravitation ceased to function, but through its union with the wood, it has been mastered by a stronger law, the law governing floating bodies, and has been emancipated from the downward pull of gravitation.
>
> — J. Oswald Sanders*

13. What do you notice in these passages about the Holy Spirit leading us?

John 14:25-27

---

* J. Oswald Sanders, *The Holy Spirit and His Gifts* (Grand Rapids, MI: Zondervan, 1940), 57.

John 16:7-8

John 16:12-15

14. What does the Holy Spirit use to communicate truth?
(Ephesians 6:17)

15. Read Hebrews 4:12-13. How do you feel about this level of expo-
sure? How could the Holy Spirit use this in your life?

16. How else does the Holy Spirit come alongside and help us? (Romans 8:26)

17. In Acts 1:8, Jesus used the expression "you will" twice. He was describing what would happen when the Holy Spirit came on the disciples.

    a. What two statements does He make?

    b. How have you experienced the Holy Spirit empowering or strengthening you?

c. How does the Holy Spirit help you in sharing Jesus and conversing about your faith?

18. Review questions 9-17. What assures you that the Holy Spirit lives in you? What impact has the Holy Spirit had on the way you lived this past week?

THE FILLING OF
THE HOLY SPIRIT

19. What do you notice about being filled by the Holy Spirit?
    (Acts 13:52 and Ephesians 5:18)

The Spirit-filled life is:

- *A lifestyle of obedience to the Holy Spirit*
  (questions 11,12)
- *A lifestyle centered on the person of Jesus Christ*
  (questions 4,8)
- *A lifestyle founded on God's living word*
  (questions 14,15)
- *A lifestyle of prayer*
  (questions 6,16)
- *A lifestyle of fellowship*
  (question 20)
- *A lifestyle that reflects and shares Jesus*
  (questions 17,20)

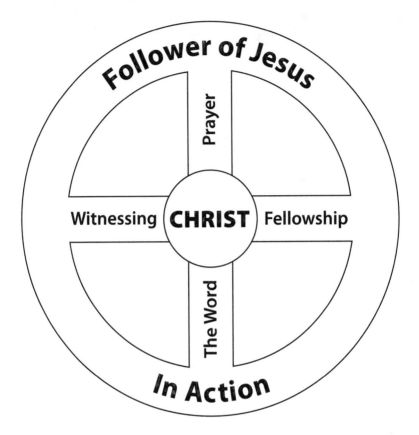

The Wheel Illustration is a helpful way to remember these basic truths about the Spirit-filled life. It is a Christ-centered life. The Holy Spirit focuses your attention on **Christ** and empowers you to live a life of **obedience** to Him. **God's Word** and **prayer** build you up in a relationship with Christ so He can live through you and reach others through **fellowship** and **witnessing.** The Holy Spirit uses each process to accomplish God's purposes and help us grow.

20. Read Acts 4:31-35. List examples of the principles from the Wheel that are reflected in the way the disciples lived.

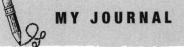

As you reflect on the work of Christ and the indwelling Spirit, do you feel worthy of receiving the grace of God? Does receiving the Spirit of God who indwells you seem scary or comforting? Express how this might affect your relationship with God.

▶ Jesus Christ promised that after He left He would prepare a place for believers and send the Holy Spirit as our helper.

▶ From His place at the right hand of God, Christ reigns over all creation and the church.

▶ He is constantly praying for His followers and building up their faith.

▶ Today the Spirit comes to live in, lead, and fill every believer.

▶ The Holy Spirit gives us power to lead an obedient, Christ-centered life.

The Holy Spirit is a Person of the Triune God and has personality. The verses below may deepen your heart's grasp of who the Holy Spirit is. Choose the ones that interest you most. Ponder the verses provided, and then jot down your response.

The Holy Spirit	Reference	What Does This Mean to You?
Prays	Romans 8:26	
Speaks	Acts 13:2	
Teaches	Romans 8:27	
Loves	Romans 15:30	
Thinks	1 Corinthians 2:10-11; Romans 8:27	
Wills	1 Corinthians 12:11	
Leads	Romans 8:14	
Can be resisted	Acts 7:51	
Can be tested or provoked	Acts 5:9	
Can be insulted	Hebrews 10:29	
Can be blasphemed	Matthew 12:31-32	
Can be grieved	Ephesians 4:30	
Can be suppressed	1 Thessalonians 5:19	

The essential BIBLE STUDY series for twenty-first-century followers of Christ.

DFD 2
The Spirit-Filled Follower of Jesus · · · · · 978-1-60006-005-2
Learn what it means to be filled by the Spirit so that obedience, Bible study, prayer, fellowship, and witnessing become natural, meaningful aspects of your life.

DFD 3
Walking with Christ · · · · · 978-1-60006-006-9
Learn five vital aspects to living as a strong and mature disciple of Christ through this easy-to-understand Bible study.

DFD 4
The Character of a Follower of Jesus · · · · · 978-1-60006-007-6
This insightful, easy-to-grasp Bible study helps you understand and put into action the internal qualities and values that should drive your life as a disciple of Christ.

DFD 5
Foundations for Faith · · · · · 978-1-60006-008-3
This compelling Bible study will help you get a disciple's perspective on God, His Word, the Holy Spirit, spiritual warfare, and Christ's return.

DFD 6
Growing in Discipleship · · · · · 978-1-60006-009-0
This study will provide insight and encouragement to help you grow as a true disciple of Christ by learning to share the blessings you've received from God.

DFD 7
Our Hope in Christ · · · · · 978-1-60006-010-6
In this study of 1 Thessalonians, discover how to undertake a comprehensive analysis of a book of the Bible and gain effective Bible study principles that will last a lifetime.

DFD Leader's Guide · · · · · 978-1-60006-011-3
The leader's guide provides all the insight and information needed to share the essential truths of discipleship with others, whether one-on-one or in small groups.

To order copies, call NavPress at 1-800-366-7788 or
log on to www.navpress.com.